Cuban Refugees

A Proud Heritage The Hispanic Library

Cuban Refugees

Cuban Roots, American Freedoms

Deborah Kent

Content Adviser: Maria R. Estorino
Project Director/Archives
Cuban Heritage Digital Collection
University of Miami Libraries
Coral Gables, Florida

Published in the United States of America by The Child's World®
PO Box 326 • Chanhassen, MN 55317-0326 • 800-599-READ • www.childsworld.com

Acknowledgments
The Child's World®: Mary Berendes, Publishing Director

Editorial Directions, Inc.: E. Russell Primm, Editorial Director; Pam Rosenberg, Project
Editor; Katie Marsico, Associate Editor; Matt Messbarger, Editorial Assistant; Susan Hindman,
Copyeditor; Lucia Raatma, Proofreader; Stephen Carl Vender, Fact Checker; Timothy Griffin/
IndexServ, Indexer; Dawn Friedman, Photo Researcher; Linda S. Koutris, Photo Selector

Creative Spark: Mary Francis and Rob Court, Design and Page Production

Cartography by XNR Productions, Inc.

Photos
Cover: Cuban refugees arrive in Miami in 1967, AP/Wide World Photos

AP/Wide World Photos: 17, 19, 20; David Adame/AP/Wide World Photos: 25; John McGawan,
Jr./AP/Wide World Photos: 30; Jacques Langevin/AP/Wide World Photos: 31; Jose Luis
Magana/AP/Wide World Photos: 35; Diaz/Corbis Sygma: 7; Reuters/Corbis: 9; Steve Starr/
Corbis: 11, 34; Bettmann/Corbis: 15, 16, 23, 29, 32; Hulton Deutsch Collection/Corbis: 21; Nik
Wheeler/Corbis: 26; Jose Luis Pelaez, Inc./Corbis: 27; Tony Arruza/Corbis: 28; Getty Images
News: 8; Hulton|Archive/Getty Images: 24; Time & Life Pictures/Getty Images: 10, 14.

Library of Congress Cataloging-in-Publication Data
Kent, Deborah.
  Cuban refugees : Cuban roots, American freedoms / by Deborah Kent.
    p. cm. — (A proud heritage)
  Includes bibliographical references and index.
  ISBN 1-59296-382-X (Library Bound : alk. paper) 1. Cuban Americans—Juvenile literature.
2. Refugees, Cuban—United States—Juvenile literature. I. Title. II. Proud heritage (Child's
World (Firm))
  E184.C97K46 2005
  973'.04687291—dc22   2004018044

Chapter One

Elian, the Miracle Boy

On November 25, 1999, a Coast Guard crew found a six-year-old boy clinging to an inner tube in the stormy waters off the coast of Florida. Days before, the boy had set off with his mother and 12 other people from the island nation of Cuba. Traveling on a poorly built raft, they tried to reach the Florida coast, 90 miles (145 kilometers) away. The inner tube was all that remained of the raft. The boy, Elian Gonzalez, was one of only three survivors of the tragic journey.

Elian went to live with an uncle in Miami, Florida. He enjoyed his new life in Miami and discovered the delights of television programs, video games, and ice-cream cones. Elian's uncle wanted him to stay in the United States. However, back in Cuba, Elian's father insisted that the boy should come home. He wanted to raise his son in the land where he had been born.

Elian Gonzalez rides a bike at his uncle's home in Miami.

The Cuban community in Florida rallied in support of Elian's uncle. Cuban Americans argued that Elian and his mother had fled from an **oppressive** government. They had risked their lives to find freedom and opportunity in the United States. Now that he was here, Elian should be allowed to stay.

In the months that followed, newspapers around the world carried the story of Elian Gonzalez. Reporters called him "the Miracle Boy" because of his amazing survival. Government officials and concerned citizens debated his future. Even Bill Clinton, president of the United States, discussed Elian with the press. Finally, the U.S. Department of Immigration and Naturalization Service (INS) reached a decision. The INS was the department of the federal government that dealt with

The Gonzalez family watches President Bill Clinton on TV after the decision was made to send Elian back to Cuba to live with his father.

immigrants at that time. It ruled that Elian should leave the United States and live with his father in Cuba.

The Cuban community in the United States was passionate in its belief that Elian Gonzalez should be allowed to remain in Florida.

Why did Elian Gonzalez and his mother brave the open sea on a raft? Why were they and their fellow rafters so desperate to reach the United States? Why did Florida's Cuban community care so passionately about Elian's fate? Why did the U.S. government grow so concerned, and why did the media shower so much attention on one little boy? The answers to these questions lie in the history of Cuba and its relationship with the United States.

Elian Gonzalez was a Cuban refugee. A refugee is someone who flees from his or her country to escape unbearable social or political conditions. Tens of thousands of Cuban refugees have come to the United States since 1959, when a revolution in Cuba established a

Communist government under Premier Fidel Castro. Many Cubans feel that life under Castro is filled with unbearable hardships. One of these is not being allowed to leave the country. Hoping to build a new life, they are willing to take their chances on the high seas.

In the early years of Castro's government Cuban refugees received a warm welcome in the United States. Their presence served as proof that Castro was a cruel leader. It told the world that the United States was a land where freedom flourished. The flight of the refugees strengthened America's position during a troubled period called the Cold War. The Cold War was a decades-long struggle between the Communist government of the Soviet Union and the capitalist, or free enterprise, system of the United States. The story of the Cuban refugees is

Fidel Castro organized a rebellion against the Cuban government in the 1950s. In 1959, he became the leader of the Communist government of Cuba.

bound up with the story of the United States in the Cold War.

But, over the years, the United States has shifted its attitude toward refugees from Cuba. During the late 1990s and early 2000s, refugees were often turned away from American shores. As a result, while he held tightly to his floating inner tube, Elian Gonzalez was tossed by the waves of the Atlantic and pounded by the forces of history.

Cuban refugees often make their way to the United States on makeshift rafts and inner tubes.

Chapter Two

Across the Straits

Cuba is separated from the United States by the **Straits** of Florida, a 90-mile (145-km) waterway that connects the Gulf of Mexico with the Atlantic Ocean. Cuba is a beautiful island with sandy beaches, rocky coves, and forest-covered hills. Its people love music, dancing, and festivals. Despite its beauty, however, Cuba has never been a paradise. Its history is marked with cruelty, greed, and sorrow.

Spain claimed the island of Cuba soon after Columbus stepped ashore in the Americas. For more than 300 years, Cuba existed as a Spanish colony. Rich Spanish families ran large plantations, where they raised sugar and other crops. Thousands of Africans were brought to Cuba as slaves to work in the fields.

In 1868, Cuba launched a struggle for independence from Spain that lasted for 20 years. The United

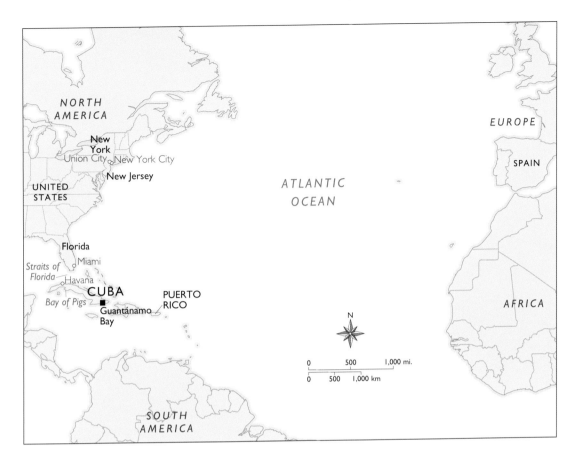

Spain claimed the island of Cuba in 1492 and controlled it from across the Atlantic Ocean until 1898. That year, the United States helped Cuba break free from Spanish rule.

States entered the conflict in 1898 and helped drive Spain out of Cuba forever. But once Spain was gone, Cuba did not immediately become a free nation. Instead, the American flag flew over the island for four years. A treaty finally gave Cuba its independence in 1902. However, the United States kept a naval base on Cuban soil at Guantanamo Bay. More than a century later, Guantanamo Bay remains in U.S. hands.

In March 1898, the *Maine,* a U.S. warship, was docked in Havana Harbor. Suddenly, a mysterious explosion ripped through the ship's hull, sinking her to the bottom. The United States blamed Spain for the explosion and used it as an excuse to go to war.

Spain once held a mighty empire in the Americas but, by 1898, had lost most of its territory. In the Spanish-American War, the United States stripped Spain of its last possessions—the Philippines, Puerto Rico, and Cuba. During the fighting, U.S. troops shouted the war cry, "Remember the *Maine*!"

Problems burdened the **Republic** of Cuba from the start. The government was unstable, and dishonesty was widespread. In 1952, a dictator named Fulgencio Batista seized control of the country. He set aside the Cuban constitution and used the military to enforce his will. A politician named Fidel Castro organized a rebel army in the mountains. Little by little, Castro's forces gained control of the countryside. Batista hung on in Havana, the capital. At last, he knew he was beaten. On December 31, 1958, he boarded a plane and fled to the United States. Castro seized power on New Year's Day 1959.

At first, Castro was wildly popular with the Cuban people. In passionate speeches, he promised to help the poor of the nation. He would build schools and hospitals all over Cuba. Most important of all, he would restore peace and order. He would punish those who had supported Batista's government and would make sure they never returned to power again.

Fulgencio Batista was the ruler of Cuba from 1933 to 1944. He seized power again as a dictator in 1952 and controlled the country until Castro forced him out in 1959.

Castro set to work at once. He ordered Batista's supporters thrown into prison or put to death. He took land from the wealthy and drove out foreign-owned businesses. Anyone who challenged him was in danger. Castro called himself the *lider maximo*, the "maximum leader," of the Cuban nation.

The new Castro government had strong backing from the Soviet Union. The Soviet Union was created in 1917 when Russia underwent a Communist revolution.

Power to the People

Communism is a system of government based on the ideas of a 19th-century German writer named Karl Marx (right). Marx saw Communism as a people's movement that would erase the differences between rich and poor. The Communist Revolution in Russia led to the overthrow of the czars, powerful emperors who had ruled for hundreds of years. The new Communist government put an end to private businesses. Everyone had to work for the government, which had enormous power. Questioning or criticizing the government was strictly forbidden.

Fidel Castro imposed a Communist government on the people of Cuba.

When Castro took over Cuba, the United States and the Soviet Union were the two most powerful nations on earth. These two superpowers also were locked in the Cold War. Each worked to spread its own system of government around the

U.S. president John F. Kennedy (right) and Soviet premier Nikita Khrushchev met in Vienna, Austria, in 1961.

world. Though no shots had been fired between the two nations, people around the world lived in fear that the Cold War would someday explode into horrifying bloodshed.

Because Castro allied himself with the Soviet Union, the U.S. government viewed him as an enemy. Communist Cuba glared at the United States across the Straits of Florida, and the United States glared back.

Chapter Three

Flight from the Homeland

"It was Halloween night when I arrived in Miami with my wife and my one-year-old son," recalled Carlos Arboleya, a Cuban lawyer. "We found a room in a house with an old lady—$5 a week was our room, one bed, all three of us slept in the one bed. But at last we were in the land of freedom and democracy and opportunity."

Like thousands of their countrymen, the Arboleyas fled to the United States soon after Castro came to power. They were part of the first wave of Cuban refugees. More than 200,000 Cubans came to the United States between 1959 and 1962. Most of these early refugees belonged to the upper and middle classes of Cuban society. The newcomers from Cuba were doctors, lawyers, teachers, and businesspeople. These individuals were the most highly educated group

In April 1961, a brigade of Cuban refugee soldiers landed at a swampy inlet on Cuba's coast. The landing place was known as the Bay of Pigs. The soldiers, who belonged to Brigade 2506, had trained for months in Guatemala. With the help of U.S. air power, they hoped to overthrow Fidel Castro.

Castro received advance warning about the invasion and went into action. He arrested some 100,000 Cubans he suspected of plotting against him. He sent troops to attack the invaders at the Bay of Pigs. The United States did not send the massive air support that the invaders had counted on. After three days of fierce fighting, Brigade 2506 suffered a crushing defeat.

Cuban refugees arrive in Miami, Florida, in 1965.

of immigrants ever to come to the United States. They were not allowed to take money and possessions out of Cuba, but they brought their knowledge and experience.

To the American public, the Cuban refugees were heroes. They had left their homeland to escape the menace of Communism. Because so many of the refugees were well educated, Americans believed they would readily contribute to their adopted country. Churches, schools, civic organizations, and the federal government reached out helping hands. Refugees received training, scholarships, loans, and some found well-paying jobs. Monsignor Bryan Walsh, a priest

Traveling Solo

About 14,500 of the early refugees were children traveling alone. They waited in foster homes until their parents were able to leave Cuba and

join them. Fourteen-year-old Maria Flores, living in a foster home in New Jersey, wrote about her experience in her high school newspaper: "My brother and I left Havana together by plane. They told us we could not take anything valuable out of the country. Our parents did not want us to go without money. I cut the string of a pearl necklace and sewed the pearls into the hem of my skirt."

who worked with refugees in Florida, wrote, "Never in the history of the United States did any immigrant or refugee population receive the kind of help that was made available to the Cubans during their early years here."

In general, the refugees did not expect to make the United States their **permanent** home. They hoped that Castro would be overthrown so that they could return to Cuba. Some refugees even prepared to launch an armed assault on the Castro government. The Central Intelligence Agency (CIA) of the United States aided them in their preparations. It provided them with weapons and military training.

On October 22, 1962, U.S. president John F. Kennedy addressed the American people. His televised speech shocked the nation and the world. Kennedy explained that the Soviet Union had begun to set up nuclear missiles in Cuba. The missiles were aimed across the Straits of Florida at the United States. Kennedy announced that the United States would not allow the Soviets to leave these weapons in place. If the Soviets continued their arms buildup in Cuba, Kennedy warned, the United States would attack.

The Cuban Missile Crisis was a showdown between the world's superpowers. Nuclear war between the

President John F. Kennedy announces that the Soviet Union has begun to set up nuclear missiles in Cuba.

United States and the Soviet Union was a terrifying possibility. For three days, the world waited in breathless fear. At last, the Soviet leader, Premier Nikita Khrushchev, agreed to **dismantle** the missiles. In return, the United States promised not to invade Cuba in the future.

A catastrophic war had been avoided, but for the Cuban refugees, relief mingled with bitter disappointment.

The refugees set aside their last hopes that the United States would help remove Castro from power.

No longer could they plan for a swift return to Cuba. They realized they would have to stay in the United States for a long time. Maybe they would never be able to go home at all. Now it was time to build a new life in the United States.

The Cuban refugees settled in cities and towns all over the United States. Many moved to New York City. A large group became established in Union City, New Jersey. The greatest number made South Florida their new home. Of these, the majority settled in Miami. They found cheap housing in a run-down section surrounding Miami's Eighth Street, *Calle Ocho* in Spanish. The Cubans called the neighborhood *La Pequena Habana,* which means "Little Havana" in Spanish. To the non-Cubans of

Fidel Castro and Nikita Khrushchev pictured together in 1960.

Cuban Americans march in a rally in Miami, Florida, in 2003.

Miami, the neighborhood surrounding Eighth Street came to be known as Little Havana.

The Cubans opened shops and offices along Calle Ocho. They bought their meat and vegetables from Cuban grocers. If they were ill, they went to Cuban doctors. If they needed to borrow money, Cuban banks were there to arrange loans. "If we had been scattered around a big city, we would have been lost," explained Luis Botifoll, a Cuban American banker. "Our businesses

Cuban American dancers participate in a parade at the Calle Ocho Festival in Miami.

thrived because our own people provided them with loyal clients and employees."

For the most part, the Cuban refugees were highly successful in the business world. They were eager to prove that they could prosper under the free enterprise system in the United States. "Castro was calling us 'worms' and 'the scum of the earth' [for leaving Cuba]," one refugee remembers. "There was a sort of silent code, or effort to say, wherever I am, I am going to demonstrate that I am a Cuban and that I am very good at what I do."

Often several Cuban families crowded into one tiny apartment. In the evenings, they gathered on the sidewalks to exchange news and share memories of their homeland. As time passed, some non-Cubans came to resent the refugees. They complained that the refugees were loud and pushy, that they took unfair advantage of American generosity. Some landlords posted signs that read "No children, no pets, no Cubans."

After the Cuban Missile Crisis, Fidel Castro forbade Cubans to leave the island. Thousands of families were cruelly divided. Husbands waited in the United States to be joined by their wives. Children in foster families prayed

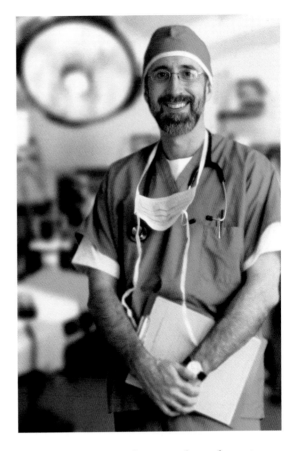

Many Cubans who sought refuge in the United States during the 1960s were successful professionals such as doctors and lawyers.

27

for the safety of parents back home. Thousands of refugees managed to leave Cuba and enter the United States illegally—without the papers that the government considered necessary.

In 1966, President Lyndon B. Johnson signed a law called the Cuban Adjustment Act. The law made it easier for Cuban refugees to apply for U.S. citizenship. Even those who had arrived illegally were **eligible.** No other immigrant group was granted such privileges.

A family enjoys a meal at a restaurant in Miami's Little Havana neighborhood.

In 1965, Castro again allowed Cubans to leave the country. From 1965 until 1973, small planes making what became known as Freedom Flights brought refugees from Cuba to Florida every day. Miami's Cuban community overflowed the borders of the Calle Ocho neighborhood. As they became more prosperous, Cubans moved to the Miami suburbs. The more the Cuban community flourished in South Florida, the more attractive it became to Cubans who had settled elsewhere. Many Cubans

Lyndon B. Johnson became president of the United States when John F. Kennedy was assassinated on November 22, 1963. He served as president until 1969.

left northern cities and moved to the Miami area.

Castro abruptly put a halt to flights from Cuba to Florida in 1973. His decision stopped the flow of refugees to the United States. Then in 1979, he began allowing refugees living in the United States to make short visits to their homeland. Thousands of Cuban

Cuban refugees board a boat in Havana, Cuba, to travel to the United States.

Americans made the journey from one world to another. Though Castro had improved literacy and health care, people on the island had few luxuries. The Cuban Americans brought dazzling gifts—cassette recorders, cameras, watches, toys, and new clothes.

More than ever before, Cubans on the island hungered to move north to the land of plenty. Castro was alarmed and embarrassed by the rising discontent of the Cuban people. To get rid of possible troublemakers, Castro invited Cuban Americans to come by boat and take away anyone who wished to go.

Cuban Americans rushed to help their countrymen who wanted to escape Castro's regime. Renting or borrowing boats of every description, they crossed the Straits of Florida to the Cuban port of Mariel. Castro and his supporters had selected the people who would be permitted to leave. Many were family members of people already living in the United States. Others were artists, writers, and musicians who expressed their discontent with the government. Some people had

Cuban refugees at the port of Mariel wait for their ship to set sail for the United States in 1980.

Cuban refugees wait excitedly for immigration officials to allow them to enter the United States.

psychiatric disabilities or were convicts. The Castro government was happy to be rid of them and delighted to make them the responsibility of the United States.

For five months, the Mariel Boatlift of 1980 brought 125,000 Cuban refugees to the United States. Most of them settled in South Florida. Their sheer numbers placed a burden on the schools and hospitals. A drastic housing shortage left many people on the streets. The arrival of so many hardened criminals triggered a crime wave. President Jimmy Carter declared a state of emergency in South Florida and gave the state $10 million to help settle the new refugees.

The flood of *Marielitos* changed the image of the Cuban refugee in the American mind. Once the refugees had been gallant heroes. Now they were problems, threats to society. The Cuban Americans struggled to regain the respect of their adopted nation.

Chapter Four

The Next Generation

Ever since Castro's takeover, the Soviet Union had given economic support to Cuba. That support disappeared when the Soviet Union's Communist government collapsed in 1990. In Cuba, the impact was disastrous. People had lived without luxuries for decades. Now even food, clothing, and other basic necessities grew scarce.

To the United States, the Soviet collapse meant an end to the Cold War. The United States emerged as the world's only superpower, free from the fear of a Soviet attack. The end of the Cold War also brought a dramatic shift in U.S. policy toward Cuban refugees. No longer were they viewed as political exiles, fleeing an oppressive government. Now, like immigrants from dozens of other countries around the world, they were seen as poor people desperate for a better future.

A Cuban refugee is interviewed by a U.S. Coast Guard official after her arrival in the United States.

In the early 1990s, Cubans began leaving the island in even greater numbers. They headed across the Straits of Florida in anything that would float. Some rode in fishing vessels or leaky rowboats; some used homemade rafts of planks and inner tubes. At first, Castro arrested anyone caught trying to leave. In 1994, he changed his policy and told the Cuban people that anyone who wanted to leave was welcome to go.

The flood of new refugees led President Bill Clinton to change a longstanding U.S. policy. Refugees from

Cuba would no longer receive special treatment. They would have to follow legal procedures like immigrants from any other country. Under this policy, 20,000 Cubans could enter the United States each year.

The U.S. Coast Guard stops hundreds of boats and rafts off the Florida shores and sends their passengers back to Cuba. However, if the refugees manage to reach U.S. soil before they are caught, they are usually allowed to stay. This confusing situation is sometimes called the "wet foot, dry foot" policy.

In Miami and other American cities, the Cuban American community continues to flourish. People of Cuban heritage have made contributions to every aspect of American life. They are teachers, artists, doctors, business owners, and politicians. Most Cuban Americans remain very conscious of their Cuban identity. They continue to hope for a new, more open government to prevail in Cuba. They help new arrivals from the homeland and sometimes rescue the rafters making the dangerous journey across the straits.

Singer Gloria Estefan is one of the many Cuban Americans who have made great contributions to American society.

In 1991, Jose Basulto, a Cuban from Miami, founded Brothers to the Rescue. The organization searches for and rescues Cubans who are trying to reach the United States by sea. Brothers to the Rescue has saved countless lives. In 1996, Castro's forces shot down two Brothers to the Rescue planes over Cuban waters. Four of the rescuers were killed.

In many ways, the story of the Cuban refugees is like the story of any group of immigrants to the United States. The Cubans left a situation they could no longer endure and came to the United States to begin a new life. During the first years, American policy gave them unique advantages.

But their achievements are also due to their own drive and their solid sense of community. "It was like taking a segment of one society and putting it in another place," explains Margarita Ruiz, a Miami radio personality. ". . . [The refugees] brought their intelligence, their knowledge, and they worked to become prosperous again. . . . They constructed a community that became successful."

1511: Spain colonizes the island of Cuba.

1898: After the sinking of the *Maine,* the United States helps drive Spain out of Cuba.

1902: A treaty with the United States gives Cuba its independence. The United States maintains a naval base at Guantanamo Bay.

1952: Fulgencio Batista takes control of Cuba.

1959: Fidel Castro seizes power in Cuba. Thousands of Cuban refugees flee to the United States.

1959 to 1962: More than 200,000 Cubans come to the United States.

1961: Refugee soldiers try unsuccessfully to overthrow Castro.

1962: During the Cuban Missile Crisis, the United States and the Soviet Union hover on the brink of war.

1966: President Lyndon B. Johnson signs the Cuban Adjustment Act.

1973: Castro halts regular flights between Cuba and Florida.

1980: Castro announces that any Cubans who wish to leave may do so from the port of Mariel and 125,000 *Marielitos* enter the United States.

1994: After a fresh flood of refugees, President Bill Clinton takes away the privileged status of Cuban immigrants.

1996: Two Brothers to the Rescue planes are shot down over Cuban waters.

1999: Six-year-old Elian Gonzalez makes international headlines.

2002: Former president Jimmy Carter meets with Castro to try to improve relations between the two countries.

Glossary

communism (KOM-yuh-niz-uhm) Communism is a system of government that discourages private ownership and establishes strong government control over industry. During the Cold War, the United States was very concerned about the spread of communism.

dismantle (diss-MAN-tuhl) To dismantle something is to take it apart. Soviet Premier Nikita Khrushchev agreed to dismantle the missiles in Cuba.

eligible (EL-uh-juh-buhl) To be eligible is to be qualified or acceptable. Under the Cuban Adjustment Act, even illegal Cuban immigrants were eligible to become U.S. citizens.

immigrants (IM-uh-gruhnts) Immigrants are people who leave their native country and move permanently to another land. Most immigrants come to the United States to escape hardships in their homeland.

oppressive (uh-PRESS-iv) Something that is oppressive holds people back and keeps them from being free. Most Cuban Americans feel that Castro's government in Cuba is oppressive.

permanent (PUR-muh-nuhnt) Something that is permanent is meant to last a very long time. At first, the Cuban refugees did not want the United States to be their permanent home.

psychiatric (sye-kee-AT-rik) Psychiatric refers to something that is related to emotional and mental health. Some of the people that Castro allowed to leave the island of Cuba were convicts and people with psychiatric disabilities.

republic (ri-PUHB-lik) A republic is an independent nation that is not ruled by a royal family. Cuba became a republic in 1902.

straits (STRAYTS) Straits are narrow passages between two landmasses. The Straits of Florida separate Cuba from the United States.

Books

Cannarella, Deborah. *Cuban Americans*. Chanhassen, Minn.: The Child's World, 2004.

Gordon, Sharon. *Cuba*. Tarrytown, N.Y.: Benchmark Books, 2003.

Hernández, Roger E. *Cuba*. Philadelphia: Mason Crest Publishers, 2004.

January, Brendan. *Fidel Castro: Cuban Revolutionary*. New York: Franklin Watts, 2003.

Stevens, Kathryn. *Cuba*. Chanhassen, Minn.: The Child's World, 2002.

Web Sites

Visit our home page for lots of links about Cuban refugees:

http://www.childsworld.com/links.html

Note to Parents, Teachers, and Librarians:
We routinely check our Web links to make sure they're safe, active sites—
so encourage your readers to check them out!

About the Author

Deborah Kent was born in Glen Ridge, New Jersey, and grew up in nearby Little Falls. She graduated from Oberlin College and received a master's degree from Smith College School for Social Work. For four years, she was a social worker at University Settlement House on New York's Lower East Side. In 1975, Ms. Kent moved to San Miguel de Allende in Mexico, where she wrote her first young-adult novel, *Belonging*. While in San Miguel, Ms. Kent helped to found the Centro de Crecimiento, a school for children with disabilities. Ms. Kent is the author of numerous young adult novels and nonfiction titles for children. She lives in Chicago with her husband, children's author R. Conrad Stein, and their daughter, Janna.

Index